THE

BRUNCH

BUNCH

A Breakfast Club Parody

By John Robison

CHARACTERS:
NARRATOR: Offstage, unseen. Can be split among any of the other actors.
BRIAN: An innocent nerd with a heart of gold.
VERNON: The principal of the school, a middle-aged bureaucrat with an ego the size of the outdoors and a failing marriage.
CLAIRE: A privileged rich girl who's better than everyone else.
BENDER: A rebel with no master. Tough exterior, tough interior, core of vulnerability.
ALLISON: Artsy and introverted, often speaks in short, sing-songy sentences
ANDREW: Wrestler through and through. Often grunts and makes other noises in reaction to others. Not smart, and often confused by life.
CARL: The janitor. Wise with no ambition.

This work was created to be a living work of art. The following script is a jumping off point, meant to be altered to local humor and for local references. Use your own comedic skills here and there to add to the comedy of this show to make it a one-of-a-kind audience experience. At the Guild Theater we performed this as a scripted reading, with the script displayed on teleprompters, which allows for moments of unscripted fun. Contact John at the address below for a digital version of this script or to discuss points of how this script might be performed.

This is a work of parody. It's based on the original work, the Breakfast Club. This is not the original work, and is not meant to be confused with the original work.

Original Cast:

BRIAN: Tim Burns

VERNON: Josh Wilder

CLAIRE: Rebecca Bost

BENDER: Zach Koehn

ALLISON: Clara Cobb

ANDREW: Ethan Hrabe

CARL: John Robison

Debuted at the Guild Theater, Lawrence, KS, March 2, 2018

THE BRUNCH BUNCH
ACT ONE

NARRATOR: Welcome to SHERMAN HIGH SCHOOL

BRIAN: Saturday detention... A fucking Saturday. What happened to the days when they'd spank students? I would welcome a good spanking right now. And then I'd have the rest of my Saturday free to play Star Wars role playing games. Nobody cares about that though. Nobody cares about my Wookie who is also a warrior when she's not a billionaire president. Nobody cares about us either. We're not actual people. We're just a brain, an athlete, a basketcase, a princess and a criminal. Maybe that's how we started out the day. But as often happens in movies from the 80s... just ONE DAY can change everything about who you are. Not that this version takes place in the 80s. But it originally came from then. You know what I mean.

<Everyone enters and sits at desks/tables. Bender leans back and puts his feet up.>
VERNON: Well...well. Here we are! Congratulations for fucking up your lives and being here on a Saturday. Doesn't matter to me. I'm getting paid time and a half today, and give zero fucks about any of you.
<Claire raises her hand.>

CLAIRE: Excuse me, sir? I think there's been a mistake. I don't belong in here with these garbage people.

VERNON: If it helps at all, I think every one of you is a piece of human garbage, you included. You're here for nine hours. No talking. No sleeping. No moving around. No mime. No planning seditious acts. No thinking sexy thoughts. And NO feet on the furniture!

<Vernon pulls the chair out from under Bender's feet. He falls hard to the ground and doesn't move>

VERNON: <kicks him with his toe.> You'll be all right. <To everyone> OK. We're gonna try something a little different today. Because I don't feel like watching you very closely, I'm going to give you an assignment. You are going to write an essay of no less than one million words, describing to me who the hell you think you are. And what gives you the right. Is that clear Mr. Bender?
<He kicks Bender a little harder. Bender stirs and groans.>

VERNON: Good. Maybe after writing a million word essay you'll get your lives together. And then you can decide if you ever want to return to Saturday detention.

BRIAN: I can answer that right now sir...That'd be "No", no for me. 'Cause I generally play role playing games on Saturday, and the rest of my team is at this very moment campaigning without me. And we have one player that WILL NOT share any of the treasure with me. Which is a shame, because I've spent the past month questing for a plus one staff of self-loathing.

VERNON: Sit down Johnson...

BRIAN: Thank you sir... He sits.

VERNON: My office is right across that hall. <points St. L> I have been experiencing some domestic issues with my partner, and I will be spending most of the day in my office crying softly, figuring out ways to keep her from divorcing me. But I will be able to see you through that open door any time I care to look. <points> Any questions?

BENDER: Yeah...I got a question. As a member of Mumford & Sons, did they give you a banjo, or did you have to bring your own?

VERNON: Making fun of the authority figure? Now you get to come back again next Saturday. How do you like that? Don't mess with the bull young man, you'll get the horns. <pause> If you upset the anthill, don't be surprised if you wake up with ants. <pause> When you turn the crank on the angry machine, be prepared for concentrated angry to drop out of the front inside a little egg. <Vernon leaves.>

BENDER: Now why would someone want to divorce that?

ALLISON: di-VORCE!
<a few quiet, uncomfortable moments>

CLAIRE: I can't believe this is happening right now...

BENDER: Oh, shit! What're we s'posed to do if we hafta take a piss?

CLAIRE: (disgusted) Please...

BENDER: I gotta be honest... My repository is already at 80-85 percent. I guess if we're stuck here... <looks around, points at books> Let's see... which author to piss on? I'm thinking we start somewhere around Bill O'Reilly.

ANDREW: You whip it out and you're dead before the first drop hits the floor!

BENDER: You're pretty sexy when you get angry...grrr!

ANDREW: Don't make me angry. You wouldn't like me when I'm angry. If I lose my temper, you're totaled man!

BENDER: Totally totaled?

ANDREW: Completely and totally totaled!

BENDER: One hundred percent completely and totally totaled?

ANDREW: You can't even total how totally totaled you will be.

CLAIRE: <interrupting> Why don't you just shut up! Nobody here is interested!

ANDREW: She is totally correct about that. Buttface!

BENDER: Well hey there Hulk Hogan! What'd you do to get in here? Did you get your dick knocked off during a match and you got all angry and threw a hissy 'cause you couldn't find it?

BRIAN: Uh, excuse me, fellas? I think we should just write our papers... a million words is kind of a lot.

ANDREW: (to Bender): Stop being a pain in the ass.

BENDER: It's a free country...

ALLISON: Freedom isn't free!!

CLAIRE (to Andrew): He's doing it to get a rise out of you! Just ignore him...

BENDER (to Claire): Better men than you have tried to ignore all this.
<gestures to his body and does a little sexy dance>

VERNON (enters): Hey! Hey! What's going on in here? Was that talking? It had better not be. I'd hate to have to unleash the beast. And when the beast gets unleashed, ain't nobody going home unscathed! <Makes a Nixon-like intimidating jowl flapping noise> Smug little pricks! <exits>

ANDREW: (to himself) Buttbag!

BENDER: I'm going to close that door. We can't have any kind of party with Vernon popping in here every few seconds.

BRIAN: Well, you know the door's s'posed to stay open. Those are the rules. We can't break rules while we're already in detention. That's just... nuts. That's like watching a Star Trek movie while wearing a Doctor Who scarf. <nerdy laugh>

BENDER: What are they going to do to us? We're already here.

BRIAN: Is there some sort of super secret double detention that the send you to? And it happens on Saturday night during the time you're supposed to be home reading books with your family? And instead of in the library, they have it in some cave under the school and you have to shovel coal all day?

ANDREW: You do know this isn't 1890, right?

BRIAN: That door is supposed to stay open.

BENDER: So what?

ANDREW: Sew buttons! You can't make decisions for all of us. There are four other people in here
you know...

BENDER: No kidding? I totally came up with a different number. Thank God you can count. See! I knew you had to be smart to be a...a
wrestle maniac.

ANDREW: You know, Bender...you don't even count. If you disappeared forever it wouldn't make any difference. You may as well not even exist at this school.

BENDER: Oh no! I don't count! Well maybe I'll just run right out and join the wrestling team then! I just want to be important. Maybe I'll also join the pep club too! Student council, photo club, excessive masturbators club, Christina Aguilera fan club, future hamburgers of America...

CLAIRE: Oh. My. God. You know why guys like you make fun of everything...

BENDER: I can NOT wait to hear the answer to this.

CLAIRE: It's 'cause you're afraid.

BENDER: How on earth did you figure it out? You're right. I'm afraid of everything. I hide behind bushes all the time because I'm so afraid of the squirrels and their beady little eyes. I can barely eat because I'm afraid of hidden spiders in my food. Fear. That's exactly why I shy away from school activities!

ANDREW: Hey! Brian feels left out! Go ahead, Brian.

BRIAN: <sheepish and proud> I'm in the math club...

ANDREW: Way to go buddy. Relevant and timely.

CLAIRE: You're afraid that they won't take you.

BENDER: Maybe I don't join in your little reindeer games because the people involved are giant assholes. Present company INcluded.

CLAIRE: You don't know us. You don't know any of us.

BENDER: Well, I don't know any militant lepers either, but I'm not gonna run out and join the Army for the Armless.

ANDREW: Brian, why don't you chime in here?

BRIAN: I'm in the physics club.

ANDREW: Good for you, buddy.

BENDER: Hey. Pinky and the Brain...do you belong to the physics club?

CLAIRE: Gag me. That's an academic club...

BENDER: So?

CLAIRE: I get enough talking about school while I'm at school. I don't need to talk about school while I'm not at school. Once I'm out of school I don't want to be learning anything new.

BENDER: (to Brian) What do you guys do in your club?

BRIAN: In physics, um, we ah, we talk about physics...about properties of physics. We experiment with physics. What makes physics work. Seeing if we can break the laws of physics. <pause> I time traveled a hamster once.

BENDER: So it's sorta social...demented and sad, but still social. Right?

BRIAN: Yeah, well, I guess you could say that. We threw a big party after we dissected the time traveling hamster.

BENDER: Dissection party. Yeah. Those are the BEST!

BRIAN: Funny story - I didn't have any shoes to wear with my physics tuxedo. So I had to borrow some shoes. And my mom freaked out because she doesn't like me to wear other people's shoes. <long pause> She had a bad experience once with her best friend's left shoe and a guy from the Internet.

ANDREW: If you guys keep talking then Vernon's gonna come back in here...I don't want to go to double detention. I got a meet this Saturday and I'm not gonna miss it because of you twatwhistles...

BENDER: Oh and wouldn't that be a tragedy! Missing a whole wrestling meet!

ANDREW: Well you wouldn't know anything about it, buttmuncher! You never competed in your whole life!

BENDER: Oh, I know...I feel all empty inside because of it. I have such a deep admiration for guys that roll around on the floor with other
guys! Secretly I wanna be just--like--you! All I I need is a lobotomy and
some tights!

VERNON: <from offstage> Principal incoming!
<Everyone quickly gets back to angelic poses, writing their papers.>
<Vernon enters, sees everyone writing, and nods, satisfied.>

That's what I fucking thought. Educator of the year here.
<He looks around, then as he exits he attempts to intimidate Bender by popping into a muscle flex pose and uttering masculine jibberish. He Exits. Bender exits after him..>

CLAIRE: What are you gonna do?

ANDREW: Drop dead, I hope!

BRIAN: Bender, that's, that's school property there...you know, it doesn't belong to us. It's something not to be toyed with.
<We hear a slam offstage. Bender comes back with a screw and runs back to his seat.>

ANDREW: Nice job. You broke the door.

BRIAN: You should really fix that!

ALLISON: SCREW!

BENDER: Everyone just shhh! I've been here before, I know what I'm doing!

VERNON <offstage>: God damnit! <enters>
Why is that door closed? That door was open. Now it's closed. Doors don't just close themselves. No. That doesn't make any sense at all. Something else is afoot. Bender. Why is that door closed?

BENDER: How're we s'posed to know? We're not s'posed to move, right?

VERNON: Who closed that door?

BENDER: Maybe a screw fell out of it...

VERNON: (to Bender) Give the screw to me.

BENDER: I don't have it...

VERNON: Screw. Me. Now.

BENDER: As appealing as that is, I'm afraid I don't have what you're looking for.

VERNON: You want me to yank you outta that seat and shake it out of you? I'll have your little body flopping around so much you'll ask me about my workout regimen so you can have muscles like mine.

BENDER: Screws fall out all the time, the world's an imperfect place...

VERNON: Come on. Give it to me, Bender...

BENDER: You really must be having troubles at home.

CLAIRE: Excuse me, sir, why would anybody want to steal a screw?

VERNON (to Claire): Watch it, young lady.

BENDER: Yeah. Don't screw with him.

VERNON: I've had enough of these misdirections and wordplay. Andrew Clark...get up here. You're going to help me put something heavy in front of it. We'll prop it open.
<They exit>

BENDER: Hey, how come Andrew gets to get up? If he gets up, we'll all get up, it'll be anarchy!

VERNON <from offstage>
Okay, now, watch the magazines!

ANDREW: <offstage> Sir, that won't...

VERNON: <offstage> Shut your cake hole, Clark. Just help me move this thing. Lift with your back.

BENDER: What if there's a fire sir? I think violating fire codes and endangering the lives of children would be unwise at this juncture in your career, sir.

VERNON: <offstage> What the hell are you doing? Twist it longways. Long Ways! Now shove at 23 degrees with fourteen joules of force. I said 23 degrees, fuck nugget! Damn it to Ice Town! Now it's fucking wedged in there! Back up. Get outta here. Back to the library with your useles ass. What's the matter with you?
<Andrew and Vernon enter.>

I expected a little more from a varsity letterman!
(to Bender)

You're not fooling anybody, Bender! The next screw that falls out is gonna be you!
<Vernon turns to leave.>

BENDER: (under his breath) Bite my ass...
<Vernon spins in his tracks and faces Bender again.>

VERNON: What was that?

BENDER: (loudly) I said bite my shiny metal ass, meatbag!

VERNON: You just bought yourself another Saturday, mister!

BENDER: <exaggerated Southern accent> Oh, Lawdy, whatever will I do now?

VERNON: You just bought one more right there!

BENDER: I'm gonna have to check my calendar!

VERNON: Good! 'Cause it's gonna be filled. You want another one? Say the word.

BENDER: Which word?

VERNON: That's another one! I've got you for the rest of your natural born life if you don't watch your step! You want another one?

BENDER: Well actually...

VERNON: You got it! Add it to the pile, pal!

CLAIRE: (worried) Cut it out! You're scaring me!

VERNON: You through?

BENDER: Well actually...

VERNON: Good! You got one more, right there!

BENDER: But I'm all done arguing.

VERNON: Another. How do you feel about that!

BENDER: How many is that?

BRIAN: That's seven including the one when we first came in and you asked Mr. Vernon here about Sanford and Son.

BENDER: Mumford & Sons.

VERNON: Now it's eight...
(to Brian)
You stay out of it!

BRIAN: Excuse me, sir, it's seven!

BENDER: Right! It's only seven!

VERNON: I have altered the deal. Pray I do not alter it further. You're mine Bender...for two months. I gotcha! I gotcha!

BENDER: What just happened?

BRIAN: That escalated quickly.

VERNON: Alright, that's it! I'm going to be right outside those doors. The next time I hafta come in here...I'm cracking skulls! Yessir. There's gonna be so much skull cracking that we're gonna need a cleanup squad for all the skull bits.
<Vernon leaves and closes the door>

ALLISON: Skull bits.

NARRATOR: An interminable amount of time later...

<Andrew is stretching. Bender is tearing pages out of a phone book. He is tossing them around.>

ANDREW: That's real intelligent.

BENDER: <over innocent> You're right...it's wrong to destroy literature...
(He continues to tear pages out.)
It's such fun to read. Old school land lines really pump my nads! <grunting> Ooh. Aaah. Nad Pumper. Who even has a land line anymore?

BRIAN: Actually my dad keeps a land line because he doesn't trust cell phones. He says they give you cancer. I think personally he's just looking for someone to blame for his cancer, but if a land line helps bring him some peace, then that's OK with me.

ANDREW: <to Claire> Hey, you grounded tonight?

CLAIRE: I don't know, my mom said I was but my dad told me to just blow her off.

ANDREW: Big party at Stubbies, parents are in Europe. Should be pretty wild...

CLAIRE: Yeah?

ANDREW: Ain't no party like a Stubbies party. Can you go?

CLAIRE: I doubt it...

ANDREW: You should come. They're going to have a live donkey with a keg strapped to its back.

CLAIRE: I don't know...

ANDREW: They're going to play all the music backward as a commentary on the music industry. It's going to be off the hook.

CLAIRE: I do like backward music...

ANDREW: They're planning to spritz all the food with a mist of turnip oil. And they're going to pump extra gluten into the air. Just ignore your mother.

CLAIRE: If I do what my mother tells me not to do, it's because my father says it's okay. There's like this whole big monster deal. It's like any minute...
Divorce... Ugh. It's exhausting just thinking about it.

BENDER: You like your old man better than your mom?

CLAIRE: They're both strict.

BENDER: No, I mean, if you had to choose between them.

CLAIRE: Talking to either one of them is like being in that episode of the Office where Michael and Jan host a dinner party. If I had a choice I'd probably go live with my brother.<small pause> In heaven.

ALLISON (loudly): Dead Brother!

CLAIRE: Shut up!

BENDER: Hey. Andre the Giant. You get along with your parents?

ANDREW: <as Andre> What are you talking about? <normal> Well if I say yes, I'm an idiot, right?

BENDER: You're an idiot either way.

<Bender turns and walks away from him. Andrew follows and pushes Bender.>

ANDREW: If we weren't in school right now, I'd hit you so hard that social workers show up at your door because your children would have bruises in the future from the me hitting you right now.
<Bender points his middle finger at the floor.>

BENDER: Can you hear this? Want me to turn it up? <Bender flips his hand around so he is now giving Andrew the bird.>
Are you cold? I'll roll this up. <rolls up his middle finger>
Want to do a shootout? <draws and fires middle fingers>
Maybe you ought to read between the lines! <Holds up three fingers>
Maybe you need some windshield wipers? <middle finger wipers>
Are you a fan of magic? <appearing/disappearing middle finger>
< Brian comes over and puts a hand on each of the guy's shoulders.>

BRIAN: Maybe we ought to take it easy on the middle finger schtick. You know, I don't like my parents either, They're total bitches. Their idea of parental compassion is just, you know, wacko!

BENDER: Hey dorkus...

BRIAN: Yeah?

BENDER: You are a parent's wet dream, okay? I can see you getting upset for them making you wear these clothes. <make fun of whatever he's wearing> But face it,
you're a Neo-Maxi-Zoom-Dweebie! What would you be doing if you weren't out making yourself a better citizen?

ANDREW: Why do you have to insult everybody? Brian's feelings are hurt now.

BENDER: I'm being honest, asshole!

ANDREW: Yeah well, Dweeb Face here has a name!

BENDER: Yeah?

ANDREW: It's Brian, and he's a very sensitive boy.

BRIAN: I'm a sensitive boy.

CLAIRE: Just leave him alone. The clothes he's wearing are fine. Just fine. Not great. But fine. I'm sure the discount rack at the Goodwill occasionally has some outstandingly average deals.

BENDER: Hey now. Let's not trash the Goodwill store. I'm sure it's not as fancy as Whole Foods, or wherever it is that you do your shopping.

CLAIRE: Whole Foods doesn't have clothes.

BENDER: Looks like Richie Rich over here shops at hoity-toity places that only sell one kind of thing. I don't know about you all, but if I can't get it at the Wal-Mart, then I don't need it.

CLAIRE: I've been to Wal-Mart.

BENDER: Recently?

CLAIRE: Gag. No. It's terrible.

BENDER: You're totally wrong. Where else are you going to find ice cream sandwiches, a bicycle and a 20-pack of underwear under the same roof?

BRIAN: It is true that Wal-Mart fills a very important niche in the economy. If people didn't like it, they'd close down.

BENDER: Plus, the people-watching is top-notch! I don't know anywhere you can see more ass crack than at Wal-Mart!

ANDREW: Is that true? People are just walking around with ass crack?

ALLISON: Ass Crack!

BENDER: Wal-Mart has it all! Muffin Top, Moose Knuckle, Cankles, Party Mullet, Camel Toe, Rocket Jaw, Cauliflower Arm, Meth Finger, Split Cleavage, Triple Nut Hangout...

ANDREW: Why have I never heard of this?

CLAIRE: It's basically a bunch of mutants stumbling around into each other.

BENDER: Come on now. Most of the people there are completely normal. The mutants are mixed in. I wouldn't expect you to know... you're too busy polishing your jewels.

<Claire gives him the finger.>

BENDER: Oh...obscene finger gestures from such a pristine girl!

CLAIRE: (resentfully) I'm not that pristine!

BENDER: Oh no? Well, are you a virgin? I'll bet you a million dollars that you are!

CLAIRE: Why don't you just shut up? You probably don't even have a million dollars.

BENDER: Have you ever kissed a boy on the mouth?
(a beat)
Have you ever been felt up? Over the bra, under the blouse, shoes off...hoping to God your parents don't walk in?

CLAIRE: It's none of your business.

BENDER: Over the panties, no bra, blouse unbuttoned, Calvins in a ball on the front seat past eleven on a school night? Played an invigorating round of Just the Tip?

ANDREW: Leave her alone!

BENDER: You gonna make me?

ANDREW: I am.

BENDER: You and what army?

ANDREW: No army. Just you and me. Just two hits. Me hitting you, you hitting the floor! Anytime you're ready, pal!
<Bender goes to hit him but Andrew gets Bender down on the ground with a wrestling move.>

BENDER: <Pained on the ground> I don't wanna get into to this with you man...

ANDREW: Why not?

BENDER: Mostly 'cause I'm all talk. I never developed any other skills or muscles. I've never needed them before. <they both get up>

CARL <enters>: Lotta noise comin' outta here. Careful. You don't want to attract the attention of AssHole McGhee. Oh, hey Brian, how you doing?

BENDER: Your dad works here?

BRIAN: He's not my dad!

CARL: I'm his uncle. I used to babysit him when he was small. Man, you could not keep clothes on that kid.

BENDER: Uh, Carl?

CARL: What?

BENDER: Can I ask you a question?

CARL: Sure. Anything I can do to expand the mind of a youngster.

BENDER: How does one become a janitor?

CARL: You wanna be a janitor?

BENDER: Fuck no. I just wanna know how one becomes a janitor because Andrew here, is very interested in pursuing a career in the custodial arts. I was wondering if it's something you plan for, or if it's something you fall into when your life plans fail.

CARL: I started out wanting to own my own convenience store. But it turns out that you have to have money before the bank will loan you money.

BRIAN: I don't think he cares, Uncle Carl.

CARL: Oh. You were making fun of me. Real nice. I just want you to know that I have keys to everything. I look through your lockers. I listen to your conversations, I read your e-mails. I spy on you in the shower. I am under the table when you're eating dinner at home with your family. I know things about you. Private things. Things you wouldn't want anyone else to know. I am everywhere. I am the night.
<Carl exits with a flourish>

ALLISON: I am the night!

ANDREW: What the fuck just happened?! Was he trying to tell us that he's Batman? Hey guys. I think he might be Batman.

NARRATOR: Much later...
<Vernon enters>

VERNON: All right my little French cheeses, that's thirty minutes for lunch...

BENDER: Uh, Dick? Excuse me, Rich...will milk be made available to us?

ALLISON: <raspy> So.... thirsty... for milk. Gonna... diiiiiie...

ANDREW: We're extremely thirsty sir...

BRIAN: I don't drink anything but milk. I also still have most of my baby teeth.

CLAIRE: I have a very low tolerance for dehydration.

ANDREW: I've seen her dehydrate sir, it's pretty gross.
<Bender stands.>

BRIAN: To say nothing of getting lots of calcium to maintain healthy bones.

ALLISON: BONES!

VERNON: There's a soft drink machine in the teacher's lounge. I'll be right back. <he exits>

ALLISON: <quietly> I fucking hate milk.

ANDREW: So, what's your poison?
<Allison doesn't answer.>

ANDREW: If you don’t drink milk, what do you drink?

ALLISON: Vodka...

ANDREW: Vodka? When do you drink vodka?

ALLISON: Most of the days.

ANDREW: A lot?

ALLISON: Days with the word day in them.

ANDREW: Is that why you're here today?
<Allison doesn't answer.>
Why are you here?

ALLISON: Why are you here?

ANDREW: Um, I'm here today because my coach and my father think I’m getting too big for my britches. They think I need to get knocked down a couple pegs. See, I get treated differently because I'm a winner.. But I'm not a winner because I wanna be one... I'm a winner because I’m better than everyone else. I got strength and speed. Kinda like a race horse. I’m a finely tuned, well-oiled machine. I’m pretty much a perfect human specimen. .

ALLISON: Barf.

BENDER: Claire...you wanna see a picture of a guy with elephantitus of the nuts? It's pretty tasty...

CLAIRE: No thank you...

BENDER: How do you think he rides a bike? Would you ever consider dating a guy like this?

CLAIRE: Can't you just leave me alone?

BENDER: I mean if he had a great personality and was a good dancer
and had a cool car...Although you'd probably have to ride in the back
seat 'cause his nuts would ride shotgun.

CLAIRE: You know what I wish I was doing?

BENDER: Op, watch what you say, Brian here is a cherry.

BRIAN: A cherry?

CLAIRE: I wish I was on a plane to France. I could by lying on a beach in the Riviera right now. Oh god. That would be sooooo amazing.

BRIAN: I'm not a cherry.

BENDER (to Brian): You're not a cherry? When have you ever gotten laid?

BRIAN: I've laid, lotsa times!

BENDER: By yourself, maybe.

BRIAN: She lives in Canada, met her at Niagara Falls. You wouldn't know her.

BENDER: Gotta love those Canadian girls. What about anyone around here?
<Brian points at Claire whose back is turned.>
Oh, you and Claire!

CLAIRE: What are you talking about?

BRIAN: (to Bender) Let's just drop it, we'll talk about it later!

CLAIRE: No! What're you talking about?

BENDER: Well, Brian's trying to tell me that in addition to the number of girls in the Niagara Falls area, that presently you and he are… riding the hobby horse!

CLAIRE: (to Brian) What kind of macho crap are you trying to pull? I thought you were better than that! Stop being a creep!

BRIAN: No! John said I was a cherry and I said I wasn't!

BENDER: What were you gesturing to Claire for?

CLAIRE: You know I don't appreciate this kind of bull shit.

BRIAN: He is lying! You know he's lying, right?

BENDER: Gaslight, party of one! Were you or were you not gesturing
to Claire?

BRIAN: Yeah, but… look. I'm sorry. I just didn't want anyone to know I'm… a virgin.

CLAIRE: Why didn't you want us to know you're a virgin?

BRIAN: Because it's personal business. It's my personal, private business.

BENDER: Well Brian, it doesn't sound like you're doing any business. Sounds like you are out of business.

CLAIRE: Ugh. It's fine to be a virgin. Whatever. Don't be a creep about it. Being misogynistic is way worse.
<Vernon enters drinking a soda>

BENDER: Righteous soda, bro. Where are ours?

VERNON: Oops. Forgot. Later, losers. <exits>

ALLISON: So thirsty. Gonna dry up and blow away…

BENDER: <to Brian> So what happened to you to make you such a pure flower? How have you lived this long without the one eyed monster ever seeing the light of day? Do you live on Sesame Street? Did your mom marry Mr. Rogers?

BRIAN: Uh, no, Mr. Johnson...

BENDER: Here's what I think ol' Bri's house is like...
(in a loud and friendly voice)
Son!
(in a kiddie voice)
Yeah Dad?
(loud)
How's your day, pal?
(kiddie)
Well Dad, did you ever have that not so fresh feeling?
(loud)
Haha. Priceless. Say son, how'd you like to go fishing this weekend?
(kiddie)
Great Dad, but I've got homework to do!
(loud)
That's alright son, you can do it on the boat!
(kiddie)
Hooray!

BRIAN: That was the best homework I ever did.

BENDER: A whole conversation and nobody even got punched in the face!

ANDREW: Holy shit dude. Is that what happens in your family?

BENDER: Oh, mine? That's real easy!
<Bender clears his throat>
(as his father)
Stupid, worthless, no good, freeloading, son of a bitch, bigmouth, know it all, asshole, jerk!
(as his mother)
You forgot ugly, lazy and disrespectful.
<Bender slams his hand back to slap his invisible mother.>
(as his father)
Shut up! Go fix me a turkey pot pie!

BRIAN: Is that for real?

BENDER: You wanna come over sometime?

ANDREW: That's bullshit. It's all part of your image, I don't believe a word of it.
<Bender comes over to Andrew and pulls down the back of his trousers to reveal a circular shaped burn on the top of his butt.>

BENDER: <quietly> What about this? Huh? Would you say that's roughly the size of a cigar? You see, this is what you get in my house when you spill paint in the garage. <pause> I don't think that I need to
sit here with you fuckin' dildos anymore!
<Bender goes to sit in the back.>

NARRATOR: Meanwhile, in Mr. Vernon's office...

VERNON: <on the phone> If you're bored, we'll spice things up. I'll bring home some fuzzy handcuffs. We'll take a ballroom dance class. We'll role play as the Vicar and the Countess. You enjoyed that a lot the last time. <feel free to riff> We'll adopt a vicious dog...

NARRATOR: And in the halls of the school...

<Bender and Claire are walking next to each other. Brian and Andrew are walking next to each other and Allison is following.>

CLAIRE: (to Bender) How do you know where Vernon is?

BENDER: I don't...

CLAIRE: Well then, how do you know when he'll be back?

BENDER: I don't. Exciting, huh? <they exit>

BRIAN (to Andrew): What's the point in going to
Bender's locker?

ANDREW: Beats me… something to do.

BRIAN: This is so stupid...Why are we risking getting caught?

ANDREW: I dunno… he'll probably be the one to get in trouble though, so why not.

BRIAN: So then what are we doing?

ANDREW: Stop asking questions. You sound like a dumbass.

BRIAN: Sorry...

<Bender enters with a bag of marijuana.>

BRIAN: That's a lot of shredded green paper!

ALLISON: Not paper!

CLAIRE: Yeah. Suspend your disbelief for a second.

BRIAN: Drugs! Marijuana! Oh! <faints>
<Bender tosses the bag to Claire and they both exit>

ANDREW: <addresses Brian> Hey buddy. Hey Brian. You don't want to be laying down on this floor. You don't know what's been down here.

BRIAN: <wakes up> Those were drugs! In school! How do you even get drugs? They're illegal!

ANDREW: It's called Colorado. Pot tourism. No big deal. Visit Denver, come home with weed. Everyone does it. Literally everyone but you. Sorry.
<Andrew exits.>

BRIAN <to Allison> Do you approve of this?

ALLISON: Better than a poke in the eye.
<She exits.>

NARRATOR: Back to the library!
<Everyone is seated. Vernon enters.>

VERNON: Bad news, you saggy Viking children. Mrs. Vernon has decided that she wants to make her own apartment out of our garage. That means the pool table has to come inside, which means I have to clear out the rumpus room. Now where am I going to have all my rumpuses?

BENDER: That sounds like a real tragedy for both you and your pool table.

VERNON: I was wondering which one of you would be dumb enough to respond. Now I get to take out all my personal frustrations on a young and impressionable student. Game on, mother fucker. <pause> Since Mr. Wiseguy here has taken it upon himself to comment on my personal situation, he'll be the target of my mayhem for the next few minutes, until I tire of his cowardly screams.

BENDER: Big talk from a guy with no place to rumpus.

VERNON: Everything's a big joke, huh Bender? The false alarm you pulled yesterday. False alarms are really funny, aren't they...What if your dope was on fire?

BENDER: That's kind of the point, sir.
<Andrew laughs.>

VERNON (to Andrew): You think he's funny? You think this is cute? You think he's bitchin', is that it? That he's a real "cool guy?" That he's the cat's pajamas? You think Bender here is the bee's knees? You probably think he's the next Wilma Flintstone. Lemme tell you something. Look at him, he's a bum. You go visit John Bender in five years! You'll see how funny he Is! About as funny as Joey Tribbiani when Friends was all done and got his own show.

BRIAN: Wait... he had his own show?

CLAIRE: Yes. It was called Joey.

BRIAN: He played the same character?

CLAIRE: Yes. That's why it was called Joey, Brian.

BRIAN: And did the other friends go with him?

CLAIRE: No, it was just him, with a whole group of new people.

BRIAN: But that would never work! He only functions when he's combined with that particular group of people! That's a recipe for disaster.

CLAIRE: And it was. How did you never hear about this?

VERNON: That's enough! No more trotting up and down the halls of the television history museum! I'm in the middle of destroying the ego of a teenager!
(to Bender)
What's the matter, John? You gonna cry? You got the weepy eyes? Got the moist balls? Come on. You're coming with me.
<Vernon grabs Bender's shoulder.>

NARRATOR: Cut to a janitor's closet!

VERNON: That's the last time, Bender. That's the last time you ever make me look bad in front of those kids. I depend on the opinions of children to keep me sane. Did you see the looks on their faces? Those kids love me. Ten years down the road they're going to send me letters to tell me what a difference I made in their lives. Some days that's all that keeps me from splattering my brains all over the cafeteria. It would be a waste of all this lean muscle mass though. Look at this. <He flexes and brings his muscles very close to Bender> It's all right. It's just fine. Don't be scared of them. You're not in any danger here, Mr. Bender. I make $31,000 dollars a year and I have a home and a pool table and I'm not about to throw it away on some punk like you… But someday, man, someday. One day you're gonna turn around, and I'm gonna be there. That's right. And that's the day I unleash the dragon. I'm gonna knock your dick in the dirt!

BENDER: Are you threatening me?

VERNON: It's not a threat. It's a promise. But what're you gonna do about it? You think anybody's gonna take your word over mine? I'm a man of respect around here. I drive a 2009 Toyota Prius hatchback. What about you? Let's find out how tough you are! Come on! I'll give you the first punch, Take your best shot! Hit me. Hit me, Bender. Please, I'm begging you! Come on, just hit me man! Just one swing… so I can feel alive. I need to feel alive, Bendy. Please… make me feel alive.
<There is a very long awkward pause>

VERNON: <quietly, embarrassed> That's what I thought...you're a gutless turd!
<Vernon exits>

BENDER: Well that was weird. Less weird than home. Still weird.
<exits around the corner and up the stairs>

NARRATOR: Back to the library!
<Bender awkwardly attempts to climb down from the stairs to the main stage area.>

CLAIRE: Oh my God! What are you doing? Where have you been?

BENDER: A naked blonde walks into a bar, with a “poodle” under one arm and a “two foot salami” under the other. She says, Give me your strongest drink. My boyfriend and I were just about to make love, when he says 'I'm gonna pound my favorite bitch with my giant sausage'. So I grabbed them both and got the hell out of there!
<Bender sits down.>

VERNON: <from offstage> I'm coming back in there, and so help me, Bender had better still be in that janitor's closet and not hiding in the library anywhere!
<Bender hides, making more noise than is necessary.>
What in God's name is going on in here? What was that ruckus?

ANDREW: Uh, what ruckus?

VERNON: I was just in my office and I heard a ruckus! I know a ruckus when I hear one! Don't even pretend I don't!

BRIAN: Could you describe the ruckus, sir?

VERNON: Watch your tongue young man, watch It! It was ruckus-y. How the hell would you describe a ruckus?

ANDREW: What is a ruckus exactly?

BRIAN: It's like a loud chaotic noise.

CLAIRE: Really, sir, there wasn't any noise…

ANDREW: But was there a ruckus?

ALLISON: Ruck! Ruck-a-cucka!

ANDREW: How ruckusy of a ruckus does it have to be?

VERNON: Stop saying ruckus! The word has lost all meaning! I will not be made a fool of! That's what home is for! <exits>

BENDER: So, Moll Flanders...Kybo Mein Doobage...
<Claire gives Bender his bag. Bender turns and walks away.>

ANDREW: Yo waste-oid...you're not gonna blaze up in here! This is a drug free school zone. It's a place for children and their approved service animals.

BENDER: Watch me.

NARRATOR: Ten minutes later…
<dancing and acting super wasted>

CLAIRE: <coughs> I'm going to die! From being awesome. Watch me dance everyone. Watch me dance and wish you were me.

BENDER: Smoke is all I need for nutrition. I will eat all the smoke. I will pass the smoke through my intestinal tract and become a rocket man!

BRIAN: Today I am a bird. A bird of death and flowers. CA-CAW!!

CLAIRE: Do you know how popular I am? I'm so popular, everybody loves me so much… I wish I had a coin with my face on it so you could all take it everywhere you went. Then you wouldn't miss me so much, Brian. You wouldn't miss me anymore.

ALLISON: <dances through> Lalalalalalala

ANDREW: This is not what happens when you smoke weed. Why is everyone acting this way?

BENDER: Oh no! Baby is fussy! Don't worry baby. Mama will take care of you. Maybe you need a feeding. Let me unbutton my shirt.

ANDREW: Fuck that.

BRIAN: I'm so high right now. <notices audience> Wait. Who are all these people? <to audience member> Did you get detention too? Wait. <looks around> Is our whole school in a warehouse or something? <to a different audience member> What are you all watching? <have a little talk about it> I'm freaking out right now! <sits next to someone> I need you to hold me until I come back down.

CLAIRE: Brian, who are you talking to?

BRIAN: MY NAME IS <insert name of actor playing Brian>!

CARL: <enters> Looks like these kids need ten minutes or so to come down. Go walk around, have a snack and a drink, and come on back in just a few!

INTERMISSION!!!

The Brunch Bunch
Act Two

NARRATOR: To the confidential records room!
<Vernon is glancing through the confidential files.>

VERNON: I love looking through confidential files. They make me feel better about myself. Wow! Look at this! Looks like someone needs to be turned in to the Department of Mutant Affairs. I'll have to give Senator Kelly a call.

CARL <enters>: Afternoon, Dick...

VERNON: Hey Carl, how you doin'?

CARL: Good. They just came out with a new scent of Pine-Sol, so that pretty much made my whole week. Being a janitor is my life.

VERNON: I suppose it's good to have rewarding work. I wish I did.

CARL: You are an educator.

VERNON: Yeah. It sucks donkey nuts.

CARL: What I wouldn't give to be able to teach kids.

VERNON: What I wouldn't give for the freedom and satisfaction of janitorial work.
<they look at each other>

CARL: What if...

VERNON: We could trade places...

BOTH: for JUST ONE DAY!?!

<they grab arms and tremble for a moment, then are quiet. They each look at their own hands in wonder.>

CARL: Well, that didn't work.

VERNON: Just as well. I'd hate to give up all this Adonis-like beauty.

CARL: So what are you doing in here looking through these private personal records?

VERNON: Oh nothing really. I just like seeing how fucked up these kids are. You'd be surprised how many of them have had electroshock therapy. Look, Carl...these kids would be really embarrassed if they knew that I knew about their bed wetting and their fucked up parents. I would really appreciate it if if if if this would be something that, that you and I could keep between us...

CARL: You'd appreciate it?

VERNON: I'd appreciate it.

CARL: You'd appreciate it if I just swept this under the rug?

VERNON: Yes I would. I'd appreciate it.

CARL: Because I'm a janitor, and sweeping is what I do?

VERNON: Ha! Right! That's funny. You're a funny guy. You ever thought about doing comedy in front of people?

CARL: That's disgusting. Let's cut to the chase. What're you gonna do for me, man?

VERNON: Well, well what would you like?

CARL: I hear you have a pool table that needs a new home.

VERNON: How did you hear about that?

CARL: Your wife told me.

VERNON: How do you know Branillia?

CARL: Let's just say I filled up a tank that desperately needed filling.

VERNON: What does that even mean?

CARL: She ran out of gas right in front of the school last week. I filled up her gas tank.

VERNON: Oh. That's a relief.

CARL: Then we banged in the science room.

VERNON: DAMN!

NARRATOR: Back to the library!
<Andrew, Brian and Allison are on one side. Bender & Claire on the other>

ANDREW: So what's your middle name?

BRIAN: Guess...

ALLISON <like a psychic>: Your middle name is Ralph, as in "puke..."
<pause>
Your birthday is March 12th, you carry a condom with you at all times, and your social security number is...

ANDREW: Wow! Are you psychic or something?

ALLISON: Something.

BRIAN: How do you know all this about me?

ALLISON: I stole your wallet...
<She produces it in her hands and grins.>

BRIAN: No fair! Give it back!
<She does and Brian glances through it to make sure nothing is missing.>

BRIAN: This is great...you're a thief too!

ANDREW: Multi-talented!

ALLISON: What's there to steal? A two dollar bill and an expired condom?

BRIAN: Expired? They expire?

CLAIRE: You shouldn't carry a condom in your wallet anyway. All the friction can wear it out and make it completely useless. Especially if it's expired.

ALLISON: You weren't going to use it anyway. You just keep it there to seem cool. You probably found it somewhere.

BRIAN: I did! I found it at a party. How did you know?

ALLISON: I can't imagine you going into a store to buy condoms. You'd pee yourself.

ANDREW: This is the first time I've heard you talk like a normal person. What gives?

ALLISON: I have a neurological disorder.

BRIAN: No kidding?

ALLISON: Yes. I'm kidding. I just like to smash people's idea of what normal society should look like. Boom.

CLAIRE <Looking through Bender's wallet as he looks through her purse>: Are all these your girlfriends?

BENDER:I don't like to put labels on relationships.

CLAIRE: What does that mean?

BENDER: Well, some I consider my girlfriends and some I just consider...

CLAIRE: Consider what?

BENDER: How long I want to stick around after we screw.

ANDREW: This is the worst fake ID I've ever seen...
<Brian laughs.>

ANDREW: Do you realize you made yourself sixty eight years old?

BRIAN: Oh, I know... in my defense, 1950 was a really great year.

ANDREW: What do you need a fake ID for?

BRIAN: So I can vote for Libertarian candidates!

ALLISON: You wanna see what's in my bag?

BRIAN & ANDREW: No!
<Allison looks hurt and then resentful. She dumps the contents of her bag onto the couch. Lots of stuff comes out. Mostly tampons and raw potatoes. Through the rest of the show, Allison will randomly take bites out of the raw potatoes and then immediately spit them out.>

ANDREW: Holy shit! There are a lot of potatoes and tampons in there.

BRIAN: Do you always carry that many…

ALLISON:Tampons. You never know when you may have to plug up gunshot wounds, or get caught in a potato blight, and you don't want to be caught without plenty of tampons and potatoes.

BRIAN: Are you gonna be like a shopping bag lady? You know like, sit in alleyways and like talk to buildings and wear men's shoes and have a pet rat and stuff?

ALLISON: What do you mean, "gonna be?"

BRIAN: Why do you think you're going to be caught in like, major gunfire?

ALLISON: My home life is unsatisfying. My mom and dad are members of rival gangs. I sleep on the streets sometimes.

BRIAN: So you're saying you subject yourself to the violent dangers of the streets of <insert name of your city or town> to escape your house? You can't just run away and live on the street. That's just wack-a-doo.

ALLISON: I don't have to run away and live on the street...I can run away and, go anywhere… Iran, Lebanon, North Korea, Afghanistan... Now stop talking to me like you're my friends. It's disconcerting!
<Allison starts putting everything back in her purse.>

ANDREW: What's the deal?

ALLISON: There's no deal, Rowdy Roddy Piper. Forget it, leave me alone.

ANDREW: You wanna talk?

ALLISON: No! If I wanted to talk I'd say "Derr… I'm a wrestler." Go away...

ANDREW: Where do you want me to go?

ALLISON: Away!! And take your problems with you!

ANDREW: Oh, I have problems?

ALLISON: You have never had a single independent thought in your head that didn't have to do with butt cheeks. That is a problem!

ANDREW: Okay, fine...but I didn't dump my purse out on the couch and invite people into my problems. So what's wrong? What is it? Is it bad? How bad? Real bad? Real real bad? Parents? Brother? Boyfriend? Camp Counselor? Republicans?

ALLISON: Yeah.

ANDREW: Which one?

ALLISON: I said. Yeah.

ANDREW: What do they do to you?

ALLISON: Chip away at my fundamental rights as a person.

ANDREW: Yeah. That's old white guys for you.

NARRATOR: To the Records Room!
<Vernon and Carl are sitting talking.>

VERNON: What did you want to be when you were young?

CARL: When I was a kid, I wanted to be John Lennon...

VERNON: Carl don't be a silly goof! I'm trying to make a serious point here.

CARL: Who wouldn't want to be John Lennon? Knowing how to play guitar... wearing glasses... getting to hang out with Ringo as much as you want. Break me off a piece of that action. Hell. At this point I'd settle for listening to a John Lennon song. Good luck ever making that happen though, am I right?

VERNON: You know who I always wanted to be? Richard Nixon. He owned dogs, you know. What a life that must have been. <pause> You know, I've been teaching for twenty two years, and each year...these kids get more and more arrogant. These kids turned on me...they think I'm a big fuckin' joke...

CARL: It's because you're kind of a big fuckin' joke. If you were sixteen, what would you think of you, huh?

VERNON: You think I give one rat's ass what these kids think of me?

CARL: What would Richard Nixon think of you? If the two of you ever had a conversation, he probably wouldn't even erase the tapes. There's nothing wrong with these kids except that they have to grow up in the world that we made for them.

VERNON: And when I get old, they're gonna be runnin' the country. That's the thought that wakes me up in the middle of the night... that these kids are the ones that are gonna be in charge.

CARL: As long as they let me have a mop bucket full of grain alcohol every night, they can do whatever they want.

VERNON: You'd better hope they develop robotic livers before you get too old, friend.

NARRATOR: Back to the library!

ANDREW: What would I do for a million bucks? Well, I guess I'd do as little as I had to… maybe something with butt cheeks?

CLAIRE: That's boring...

ANDREW: Well, how'm I s'posed to answer?

CLAIRE: The idea is to like search your mind for the absolute limit. Like, uh, would you drive to school naked?
<Andrew laughs.>

ANDREW: I'm not really comfortable with nudity. My own or anyone else's. Would I have to get out of the car?

CLAIRE: Of course...

ANDREW: In the spring, or winter?

CLAIRE: It doesn't matter.

ANDREW: It does matter. Cold temperatures have a bad effect upon the genitals of the male. Makes things look like a shriveled up Vin Diesel.

CLAIRE: Fine. Spring then.

ANDREW: In front of the school or in back of the school?

CLAIRE: Holy crap dude. Either one. Just answer the question.

ANDREW: <thinking it over> Yes. I would do it. It wouldn't be that bad. I'm pretty hairy. People would probably just think it was a bear. I could live with that.

ALLISON: I'd get naked anywhere. For way less than a million dollars. I kind of want to strip down right now.
<They all look at her.>
I'll do anything sexual. I'm a very sex-u-al person. Madonna sent me a letter once that said, "Damn girl. You so sexual." <bites and spits a potato>

CLAIRE: What are you talking about?

ALLISON: I've already done just about everything there is. BDSM. Pegging. Juicing. Four on the Floor. The Swirling Duckling. The Three-Toed Sloth. The Rainy Day Special. Achilles Frottage. Missionary.

CLAIRE: Are those even things?

BRIAN: Are your parents aware of this?

ALLISON: The only person I told was my shrink...

ANDREW: And what'd he do when you told him?

ALLISON: The Wonky Pirate.

CLAIRE: Here we go.

ALLISON: He bent me over his couch.

BENDER: How is that the wonky pirate?

ALLISON: He was wearing an eyepatch.

CLAIRE: There it is.

ALLISON: I can't decide if it was prostitution or not since I paid him.

CLAIRE: You're only seventeen! And he's an adult!

ALLISON: Yeah...he's married too!

CLAIRE: Do you have any idea how completely gross that is?

ALLISON: Well, it felt a little strange the first few times...

CLAIRE: First few times? You mean he did it more than once?

ALLISON: Sure...

CLAIRE: Are you crazy?

BRIAN: Obviously she's crazy if she's screwing a person with an eyepatch.

ALLISON (to Claire): Have you ever done it?

CLAIRE: I don't even have a psychiatrist...

ALLISON: Have you ever done it with a normal person? Any person?

CLAIRE: Didn't we already cover this?

BENDER: You never answered the question...

CLAIRE: Look, I'm not gonna discuss my private life with total strangers.

ALLISON: It's kind of a double-edged sword, isn't it?

CLAIRE: I have no idea what you mean.

ALLISON: Well, if you say you haven't... you're a prude. If you say you have...you're a slut! To quote my uncle Akbar... “It's a trap.”

CLAIRE: Fine. I've never done it. Not that I haven't had chances. Lots of guys wanted to. But I'm just not ready yet. I'm kind of scared.

ALLISON: I was scared the first time too. But there's really nothing scary about it. Except for when you try the Angry Citadel Maneuver. That one is scary.

CLAIRE: I want to do it with someone I'm in love with. I just haven't found someone who's worth my time and energy.

BRIAN: I think that's great. I feel the same way.

ANDREW: Brian, let's not kid ourselves. If a female type person even gave you a second look you'd have to change your underwear.

<Silence for two beats.>

ALLISON: I never did it either.

CLAIRE: What!?

ALLISON: I made it all up. None of those things actually exist. There's no such thing as Missionary..

CLAIRE: You made it all up? I don't believe it!

ALLISON: Want to see my hymen?

THE OTHERS: No!, No Way!, Hey!

ANDREW: Woah. woah. Slow down. What's a hymen?

CLAIRE: I can't believe you, you're so weird. When you finally start talking like a normal person...you unload all these tremendous lies! That's just bizarre!

ANDREW: What's bizarre? Everyone is strange in their own way! Some of us are just better at hiding it.

CLAIRE: (to Andrew) How are you bizarre? You seem boring as shit.

ANDREW: Well… uh…

ALLISON: He can't think for himself...

ANDREW: <robotic> I can't think for myself. <normal again> Do you guys know what, uh, what I did to get in here?

BENDER: Did it have something to do with butts?

ANDREW: No! <pause> Yes. I taped <name of actor who plays Brian>'s butt cheeks together.

BRIAN: That was you?

ANDREW: Yeah, you know him?

BRIAN: Yeah, I know him. He's a great guy. He's sensitive, giving, happy, and single <mugs audience> He sure didn't deserve to have that happen to him.

ANDREW: Well you know how hairy he is?

BRIAN: He's not that hairy. He has an appropriate amount of coverage.

ANDREW: Well, when they pulled the tape off, most of his hair came off. They say the duct tape looked like giant mutant caterpillars.

CLAIRE: Oh my God… those are the worst kind of caterpillars.

ANDREW: The weird thing was that the whole time I was staring down at Tim's butt, I was thinking of my old man. And how he was disappointed that I never cut loose...So, I'm sitting in the locker room, and <Brian actor> is undressing a couple lockers down from me. And I was staring at his butt cheeks, thinking about my father, and the
next thing I knew... <trails off>
How do you apologize for something like that? It's all because of me and my old man. Oh God, I fucking hate him! "Andrew, you've got to be number one! I won't tolerate any losers in this family."
You know, sometimes, I wish my knee would give...and I wouldn't be able to wrestle anymore. And he could forget all about me...

BENDER: I think your old man and my old man should get together and go bowling. And then we burn down the bowling alley while they're in there. Then piss on the ashes.

BRIAN: It's like when I, when I look at myself. I mean really take a good look. And I don't like what I see.

CLAIRE: Why don't you like yourself?

BRIAN: 'Cause I'm failing shop. We had this assignment, to make a ceramic elephant lamp, and when you pull the trunk the light goes on. My light didn't go on, and I got a F on it. Never got a F in my life... When I signed up for shop I thought it would be an easy way to maintain my grade point average...

BENDER: Why'd you think it'd be easy?

BRIAN: Have you seen some of the dopes that take shop?

BENDER: I take shop.

BRIAN: I know. You're proving my point. All shop did was prove how useless I am.

ANDREW: We're all pretty useless.

ALLISON: I can write with my toes! I can also give erotic massage to a rhino, stab a hobo...

CLAIRE: With your feet?

BRIAN: I can make spaghetti! It doesn't taste good, but it gets mostly cooked!

CLAIRE (to Andrew): What can you do?

ANDREW: I can...uh...tape all your butt cheeks together...

BENDER: What can you do Claire?

CLAIRE: Forget it, it's way too embarrassing.

BENDER: We're way beyond being embarrassed now.

CLAIRE: I can't believe I'm actually doing this...
<Claire removes a candy bar from her bra. She unwraps it in an awkwardly sexy way, puts it in her cleavage and proceeds to chomp it. When she lifts her head, chocolate is smeared all over her face. Allison rushes forward and also takes a bite of it. Everyone slow claps>

ANDREW: All right, great! Where'd you learn to do that?

CLAIRE: As soon as I got boobs, I thought, I wonder if I can eat things from them. It turns out I can. My favorite thing to do is to put a turkey leg in there.

BENDER: That was great, Claire...my image of you is totally blown...Now all I can think of is you going to town on a drumstick stuck between your boobs.

CLAIRE: Shut up...

ALLISON: This is just like being at home with my parents.

ANDREW: You're right. My God, are we gonna be like our parents?

CLAIRE: Not me...ever...

ALLISON: It's unavoidable, it just happens.

CLAIRE: What happens?

ALLISON: When you grow up, your heart dies. And you get gingivitis. And dick rot.

BRIAN: Um, I was just thinking, I mean. I know it's kind of a weird time, but I was just wondering, um, what is gonna happen to us on Monday? When we're all together again?

CLAIRE: Are we still friends, you mean?

BRIAN: Yeah...

CLAIRE: I don't think so...

ANDREW: That's a real nice attitude, Claire!

CLAIRE: Be honest, Andy...if Brian came walking up to you in the hall on Monday, what would you do? I imagine he'd walk up to you and say hello, and the next thing he knows, his pants are off and you're staring right into his big brown eye.

ANDREW: No way! I'd never do that! Not to my Brian! He's nothing like <name of actor playing Brian>!

ALLISON: What if I came up to you and put my tongue in your mouth?

ANDREW: I don't know where that thing has been!

ALLISON: On every doorknob in the school, for one thing.

CLAIRE: It's the same exact thing! We wouldn't give Allison the time of day.

BRIAN: None of you would be our friends?

BENDER: Looks like you're out of luck, Neil deGrasse Tyson.

BRIAN: That means that Allison and I are the best ones in the room. My standards for friendship are very low. I'd be friends with anyone. Like my Mom. She's my best friend.

ALLISON: I don't have any friends.., only an army of silent insects, awaiting my command to take over city hall.

BRIAN: Well what if you had friends that were people?

ALLISON: The only kind of people I'd want as friends are servers at IHOP. They have access to the national strategic boysenberry syrup supplies.

BRIAN: I just wanna tell, each of you, that I would be proud to have any of you as a friend, and that you are welcome anytime at the tea parties that I have with my Mom and her sister.

CLAIRE: Let's just be honest Brian. You don't have any friends.

ANDREW: When are these tea parties?

BRIAN: You're so conceited, Claire. You're so full of yourself, why are you like that?

CLAIRE: Have you seen me? I'm gorgeous! There's a lot of pressure that goes along with that. I have to be gorgeous constantly. It's exhausting. You wouldn't understand.

BRIAN: I don't understand what? You think I don't understand pressure, Claire? Well fuck you! Know why I'm here today? Do you? I'm here because Mr. Ryan found a gun in my locker...

ANDREW: Why'd you have a gun in your locker?

BRIAN: Just forget it...

ANDREW: You brought it up, man!

BRIAN: I can't have an F, I just can't. My parents would be devastated. Even if I aced the rest of the semester, I'm still only at a B. And you can't get into <name of hated regional university with a B. Everything's ruined for me!

CLAIRE: But you can't kill yourself. You just can't.

BENDER: And you can't go to <hated university>. Can we talk about that decision?

BRIAN: Well I didn't do it, did I?
<pause>

ALLISON: You wanna know what I did to get in here? Shot down a German warplane!

VERNON: <pops in> Hey StinkFarts - you've only got a half hour left. Hope you've got your papers almost done. I'll be back in thirty... I'm on eBay and am so close to winning an autographed picture of Conrad Baines. <exits>

BENDER: Who the fuck?

BRIAN: He was the old guy on Diff'rent Strokes.

CLAIRE: Heyyyyyy Brian?

BRIAN: Yeah?

CLAIRE: Are you gonna write your paper?

BRIAN: Yeah, why?

CLAIRE: Well, it's kinda a waste for all of us to write a paper, don't you
think? I think we'd all kinda say the same thing. Maybe we should just have one and put all our names on it.

BRIAN: You are just trying to get out of writing a paper.

CLAIRE: True, but, you're the smartest of all of us, so it might as well be you, right?

BRIAN: I am the smartest out of this group by a lot. All right, I'll do it...

CLAIRE: Great... Hey. While you're doing that, I have an idea. <Grabs Allison by the hand> Come on...

ALLISON: Where're we going?

CLAIRE: Come on. Don't be afraid. I'm going to put makeup on you and make you conventionally attractive.

ALLISON: I'm sure going to miss my individuality. <they exit>

BRIAN: <recites lyrics to a song, perhaps "We Are Young" by Fun or something comparable, long enough to stall for the transformatoin happening backstage>

BENDER: Well that was fun.

BRIAN: Thank you.

BENDER: Seriously though, that's pretty dark, Johnson.

BRIAN: These are dark times.

ALLISON: <enters just as she was>

ANDREW: I thought you were getting a makeover so you were pretty in all the ways society tells me people should be pretty.

ALLISON: It didn't take. We did Claire instead.
<Claire enters. She's wearing crazy makeup and has her hair in a unique and non-traditional style>

BRIAN: Cool! Look what you did!

ALLISON: Thank you!

ANDREW: <to Claire> What happened to you?

CLAIRE: Why? Allison did it! What's wrong?

ANDREW: Nothing's wrong, it's just so different.

CLAIRE: Is that good or bad?

ANDREW: It's good.

NARRATOR: Finally, the end of the day...
<Everyone gathers their stuff. Carl enters, sweeping>

CARL: See ya at the tea party on Tuesday Brian...

BRIAN: See you then, Carl...

ALLISON: I'll be there too! I'm bringing my own oolong. And I'm not sharing.

BENDER: (to Carl) See you next Saturday Carl. I'll bring donuts...

CARL: You bet! You know Bender, you're going to make a hell of a janitor one day.
<The students all exit. Vernon enters>

VERNON: Well that was a day.

CARL: Pretty much every day is the same when you're the janitor.
<exits>

VERNON: What's this!?! One assignment completed for five people? Oh, there will be probably no consequences for this!

VERNON: <reads silently for a moment>
My goodness. That's a rather interesting narrative of an evening out.
<or other commentary based upon Brian's earlier writings>
<turns the paper over>
Wait. There's more:
Dear Mr. Vernon, we accept the fact that...

BRIAN : <offstage while Vernon mouths the words>
...we had to sacrifice a whole Saturday in detention for whatever it was we did wrong. But we think you're crazy to make an essay telling you who we think we are. You see us as you want to see us... In the simplest terms, in the most convenient definitions.
<Walks slowly across the stage, coming to the front>
But what we found out is that each one of us is a brain...
<Andrew slowly enters>

ANDREW: ...and an athlete...
<Allison enters>

ALLISON: ...and a basket case...
<Claire enters>

CLAIRE: ...a princess...
<Bender enters>

BENDER: ...and a criminal...

BRIAN: Does that answer your question?

ALL: Sincerely yours, the Brunch Bunch.
<In tandem, each of them thrusts their fists into the air in a silent cheer and freezes there for a very long time before the ending music comes in..>

The End.

About the parody artist:

John Robison is an actor/director/writer based in Lawrence, KS. He's the artistic director of the Guild Theater, also of Lawrence, KS, and spends his time teaching and performing improv, writing and performing parodies of popular television shows and movies, hosting live talk shows, and doing whatever other random creative projects come to mind. He holes up in a glorified cave with his son, Miles, and his daughter, Ivy, and the two betta fish he never bothered to learn the names of.